Soft Knittin

Knitting Baby Stuff Guide Book

Copyright © 2023

DEDICATION

Contents

I. Knit Homebody Lounger Pillow 1

II. Knit Yoke Baby Cardigan And Hat........................ 9

III. Knit Moon Baby Pillow..................................... 18

IV. Funny Bunny Blanket Hoodie 26

V. Bella & Brian Sloth 36

VI. Knit Baby Jacket Set.. 47

VII. Cutie Booties And Cap To Knit........................ 56

VII. Strawberry Set 62

I. Knit Homebody Lounger Pillow

MATERIALS

Bernat® Sheepy™ (8.8 oz/250 g; 149 yds/136 m)

Bunny Brown (43003) 4 balls

Size U.S. 11 (8 mm) circular knitting needle 36" [91.5 cm] long or size needed to obtain gauge.

Yarn needle.

One 24" [61 cm] square pillow form.

Two 12" [30.5 cm] square pillow forms.

Additional stuffing.

Optional: Stitch markers.

ABBREVIATIONS

Alt = Alternate

Approx = Approximately

Beg = Beginning

Cont = Continue(ity)

Dec = Decrease

K = Knit

K2tog = Knit next 2 stitches together

M1 = Make 1 stitch by picking up horizontal loop lying before next stitch and knitting into back of loop

P = Purl

Rem = Remaining

Rep = Repeat

RS = Right side

Ssk = Slip next 2 stitches knitwise one at a time. Pass them back onto left-hand needle, then knit through back loops together

St(s) = Stitch(es)

Tog = Together

WS = Wrong side

MEASUREMENTS

Approx 18" [45.5 cm] deep x 22" [56 cm] tall.

GAUGE

9 sts and 10 rows = 4" [10 cm] in stocking st.

INSTRUCTIONS

Notes:

• Due to dense yarn pile, place a safety pin or stitch marker on RS of work to help keep track.

• Work back and forth across needle in rows. Do not join.

FRONT

Cast on 24 sts. Beg on a knit row, work 16 rows in stocking st, ending on a purl row.

Next row: (RS). Cast on 14 sts. Knit to end of row. 38 sts.

Next row: Cast on 14 sts. Purl to end of row. 52 sts. Cont in stocking st until work from beg measures 22¼" [56.5 cm], ending on a purl row. Cast off.

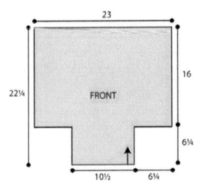

BACK

Cast on 106 sts. Beg on a knit row, work 16 rows in stocking st, ending on a purl row.

Next row: (RS). Cast off 28 sts. K1. M1. Knit to end of row. 79 sts.

Next row: Cast off 28 sts. P1. M1. Purl to end of row. 52 sts.

Cont in stocking st until work from beg measures 22¼" [56.5 cm], ending on a purl row.

Cast off.

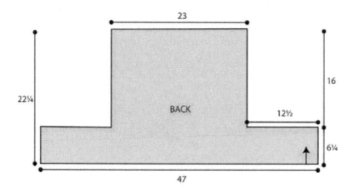

ARM FLAP (make 2)

Cast on 29 sts. Beg on a knit row, work 16 rows in stocking st, ending on a purl row.

Cast off.

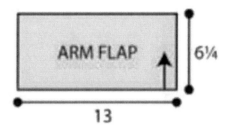

ARM GUSSET (make 2)

Cast on 16 sts. Beg on knit row, work in stocking st until work from beg measures 31" [79 cm], ending on a purl row.

Cast off.

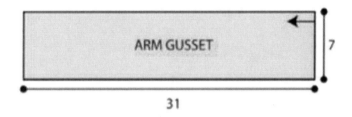

BOTTOM GUSSET

Cast on 52 sts.

1st row: (RS). Knit.

2nd and alt rows: Purl.

3rd row: K1. (ssk) twice. Knit to last 5 sts. (K2tog) twice. K1. 4 sts dec'd. 48 sts.

5th row: As 3rd row. 44 sts.

7th row: K1. (ssk) 3 times. Knit to last 7 sts. (K3tog) 3 times. K1. 6 sts dec'd. 38 sts.

9th to 13th rows: As 3rd to 7th rows. 24 sts.

14th row: Purl.

Cast off.

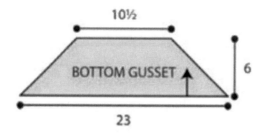

ASSEMBLY

Notes: Ensure RS (knit side) is always facing out.

Sew as indicated in Assembly Diagrams using Mattress St.

MATTRESS STITCH

With WS tog, sew Front and Back tog along red lines (A).

Sew each Arm Gusset to Back along orange lines (B).

Sew each Arm Flap to an Arm Gusset along green lines (C).

Sew rem edge of each Arm Flap to Front along blue lines (D).

Sew each Arm Gusset to Front along purple lines (E).

Sew short end of Bottom Gusset to Front along pink lines (F).

Sew long end of Bottom Gusset to Back along grey lines (G).

With WS tog, sew Front and Back tog along red lines (A).

Sew each Arm Gusset to Back along orange lines (B).

Sew each Arm Flap to an Arm Gusset along green lines (C).

Sew rem edge of each Arm Flap to Front along blue lines (D).

Sew each Arm Gusset to Front along purple lines (E).

Sew short end of Bottom Gusset to Front along pink lines (F).

Sew long end of Bottom Gusset to Back along grey lines (G).

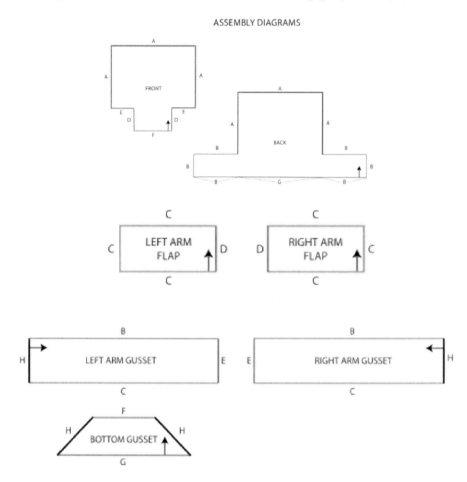

ASSEMBLY DIAGRAMS

II. Knit Yoke Baby Cardigan And Hat

MATERIALS

Bernat® Softee Baby™ (5 oz/140 g; 362 yds/331 m)

Sizes 6 12 18 24 mos

Prettiest Pink (30205) or Aqua (30201) 2 2 2 3 balls

Size U.S. 6 (4 mm) circular knitting needle 24" [60 cm] long.

Set of 4 size U.S. 6 (4 mm) double-pointed knitting needles or size needed to obtain gauge.

Stitch markers.

3 buttons.

Yarn needle.

ABBREVIATIONS

Alt = Alternate(ing)

Beg = Beginning

Dec = Decreasing

Cont = Continue(ity)

Inc = Increasing

K = Knit

K2tog = Knit next 2 stitches together

M1 = Make 1 stitch by picking up horizontal loop lying before next stitch and knitting into back of loop

P = Purl

PM = Place marker

Rep = Repeat

Rnd(s) = Round(s)

RS = Right side

SM = Slip marker

Ssk = Slip next 2 stitches knitwise one at a time. Pass them back onto left-hand needle, then knit through back loops together

St(s) = Stitch(es)

WS = Wrong side

Yo = Yarn over

SIZES

To fit chest measurement

6 mos 17" [43 cm]

12 mos 18" [45.5 cm]

18 mos 19" [48.5 cm]

24 mos 21" [53.5 cm]

Finished chest

6 mos 23" [58.5 cm]

12 mos 24" [61 cm]

18 mos 251/2" [65 cm]

24 mos 271/2" [70 cm]

Hat: Two sizes, to fit baby 6-12 (18-24) mos.

GAUGE

22 sts and 30 rows = 4" [10 cm] in stocking stitch.

INSTRUCTIONS

The instructions are written for smaller size.

If changes are necessary for larger sizes the instructions will be written thus ( ).

Numbers for each size are shown in the same color throughout the pattern.

When only one number is given in black, it applies to all sizes.

CARDIGAN

Note: Garment is worked from neck edge down.

When yoke is complete, Body is worked in one piece in rows.

Sleeves are worked in rnds on double-pointed needles.

Body

Cast on 96 (96-100-108) sts. Do not join in rnd.

Working back and forth across needle in rows, proceed as follows:

Knit 5 rows (garter st), noting 1st row is WS.

Girl's Version only:

Next row: (RS – buttonhole row). Knit to last 5 sts. ssk. yo. K3.

Boy's Version only:

Next row: (RS – buttonhole row). K3. yo. K2tog. Knit to end of row.

Both Versions: Knit 3 rows (garter st).

Note: Work 2 more buttonholes as given above on Right Front for Girl or Left Front for Boy spaced 2" [5 cm] apart.

Proceed as follows:

1st row: (RS). K7. PM. K14 (14-15- 17). M1. K13. M1. K28 (28-30-34). M1. K13. M1. K14 (15-15-17). PM. K7. 100 (100-104-112) sts.

2nd and alt rows: K7. SM. Purl to last 7 sts. SM. K7.

3rd row: K7. SM. K14 (14-15-17). M1. K1 (PM on last st). M1. K13. M1. K1 (PM on last st). M1. K28 (28-30-34). M1. K1 (PM on last st). M1. K13. M1. K1 (PM on last st). M1. K14 (14-15-17). SM. K7. 108 (108- 112-120) sts.

5th row: *Knit to marked st. M1. K1. M1. Rep from * 3 times more. Knit to end of row.

6th row: K7. SM. Purl to last 7 sts. SM. K7.

Rep last 2 rows 13 (14-15-16) times more, noting position of 2 more buttonholes. 220 (228-240- 256) sts.

Divide for Fronts, Back and Sleeves:

Next row: (RS). K7. SM. K29 (30-32-35) for Right Front.

Cast on 3 sts.

PM on 2nd cast on st.

Slip next 45 (47-49-51) sts onto length of yarn for Right Sleeve.

K58 (62-64-70) for Back.

Cast on 3 sts.

PM on 2nd cast on st. Slip next 45 (47-49-51) sts onto length of yarn for Left Sleeve. K29 (30-32-35). Sm. K7 for Left Front. 136 (140- 148-160) sts for Body.

Next row: (WS). K7. SM. Purl to last 7 sts. SM. K7.

Next row: K7. Remove marker. Knit to last 7 sts, inc 2 (4-2-2) sts evenly across. Remove marker. K7. 138 (144-150-162) sts.

Next row: (WS). K7. Purl to last 7 sts. K7.

Proceed in pat as follows:

1st row: (RS). Knit.

2nd row: K7. P4. *K2. P4. Rep from * to last 7 sts. K7.

3rd row: Knit.

4th row: K7. P1. K2. *P4. K2. Rep from * to last 8 sts. P1. K7.

Rep last 4 rows for pat until work from joining row measures 6 (7-71/2-8)" [15 (18-19-20.5) cm], ending on a WS row.

Next row: (RS). Knit, dec 4 (6-8-10) sts evenly across. 134 (138-142-152) sts. Knit 8 rows (garter st).

Cast off knitwise (WS).

Sleeves

1st rnd: (RS). With set of 4 doublepointed needles, K45 (47-49-51) sleeve sts. Pick up and knit 3 sts at underarm.

Divide sts onto 3 needles.

Join in rnd.

PM after cast on st for beg of rnd. 48 (50- 52-54) sts. Knit in rnds until work from pick up row measures 1 (1½-2-2)" [2.5 (4-5-5) cm].

Next rnd: K1. ssk. Knit to last 3 sts. K2tog. K1. Knit 7 rnds even. Rep last 8 rnds 4 times more. 38 (40-42-44) sts. Knit even in rnds until work from pick up row measures 6 (6½-7-8)" [15 (16-18-20.5) cm], dec 2 sts evenly across last rnd. 36 (38-40- 42) sts.

Next rnd: Purl.

Next rnd: Knit. Rep last 2 rnds 3 times more.

Cast off purlwise.

FINISHING

Pin garment to measurements. Cover with a damp cloth, leaving cloth to dry. Sew buttons to correspond to buttonholes.

HAT

With set of 4 double-pointed needles, cast on 85 (90) sts. Divide sts onto 3 needles.

Join in rnd. PM for beg of rnd.

1st rnd: Purl.

2nd rnd: Knit. Rep last 2 rnds 4 times more, inc 5 sts evenly across last rnd. 90 (95) sts. Knit in rnds until work from beg measures 4 (4½)" [10 (11.5) cm], ending on a purl row.

Shape top:

1st rnd: (RS). *K16 (17). K2tog. Rep from * around. 85 (90) sts.

2nd and alt rnds: Knit.

3rd rnd: *K15 (16). K2tog. Rep from * around. 80 (85) sts

5th rnd: *K14 (15). K2tog. Rep from * around. 75 (80) sts.

7th rnd: *K13 (14). K2tog. Rep from * around. 70 (75) sts.

Cont in this manner, dec 5 sts as established on every following alt rnd until 10 sts rem.

Break yarn, leaving a long end.

Draw end tightly through rem sts.

Pull tightly.

Fasten securely.

Pompom

Wind yarn around 3 fingers approx 60 times. Remove from fingers and tie tightly in center.

Cut through each side of loops. Trim to a smooth round shape.

Sew to end of Hat.

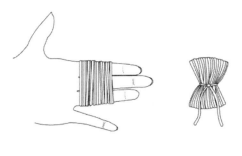

CHART

6-st rep

Key

☐ Knit on RS rows. Purl on WS rows.
⊟ Purl on RS rows. Knit on WS rows.

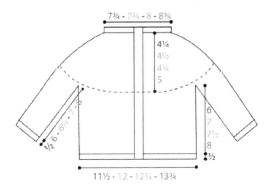

III. Knit Moon Baby Pillow

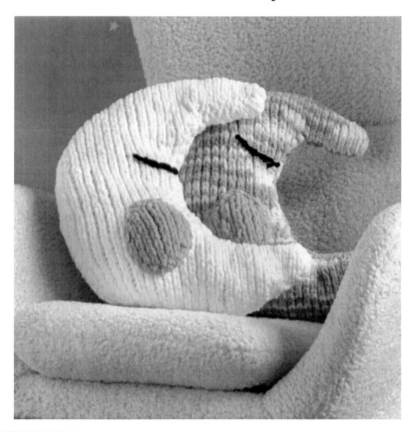

MATERIALS

Bernat® Baby Blanket Sparkle™ (10.5 oz/300 g; 220 yds/201 m)

Main Color (MC)

Moonlight Sparkle (71001) 1 ball or 98 yds/90 m Contrast A

Rose Glow Sparkle (71002) 1 ball or 12 yds/11 m Bernat® Baby

Blanket™ (10.5 oz/300 g; 220 yds/201 m)

Main Color (MC)

Baby Blue Green (04795) 1 ball or 12 yds/11 m

Size U.S. 10½ (6.5mm) knitting needles or size needed to obtain gauge.

ABBREVIATIONS

Approx = Approximately

Beg = Beginning

RS = Right side

St(s) = Stitch(es)

K = Knit

K2tog = Knit next 2 stitches together

Kfb = Increase 1 stitch by knitting into front and back of next stitch

Ssk = Slip next 2 stitches knitwise one at a time. Pass them back onto lefthand needle, then knit through back loops together

P = Purl

P2tog = Purl next 2 stitches together

Pfb = Increase 1 stitch by purling into front and back of next stitch

RS = Right side

Tog = Together

WS = Wrong side

MEASUREMENT

Approx 18" [45.5 cm] tall x 15" [38 cm] wide.

GAUGE

9 sts and 14 rows = 4" [10 cm] in stocking st.

INSTRUCTIONS

PILLOW FRONT

With MC, cast on 7 sts. Shape bottom of pillow:

1st row: (RS). Knit.

2nd row: Cast on 2 sts. Purl to last 2 sts. Pfb. P1. 10 sts.

3rd row: Cast on 2 sts. Knit to last 2 sts. Kfb. K1. 13 sts.

4th and 5th rows: As 2nd and 3rd rows. 19 sts.

6th row: As 2nd row. 22 sts.

7th row: Kfb. Knit to last 2 sts. Kfb. K1. 24 sts.

8th row: Pfb. Purl to last 2 sts. Pfb. P1. 26 sts.

9th row: Knit to last 2 sts. Kfb. K1. 27 sts.

10th row: Purl.

11th row: Knit.

12th row: Purl

13th row: Cast off 4 sts. Knit to last 2 sts. Kfb. K1. 24 sts.

14th row: Purl to last 2 sts. P2tog. 23 sts.

15th row: Cast off 4 sts. Knit to end of row. 19 sts.

16th row: Pfb. Purl to last 2 sts. P2tog.

17th row: ssk. Knit to end of row. 18 sts.

18th row: Purl to last 2 sts. P2tog. 17 sts.

19th row: Knit.

20th row: Purl.

21st row: Knit to last 2 sts. Kfb. K1. 18 sts

22nd row: As 18th row. Beg on a knit row, work 14 rows stocking st, ending on a purl row.

Shape top of Pillow:

1st row: (RS). Kfb. Knit to end of row.

2nd row: Purl.

3rd row: Knit to last 2 sts. K2tog.

4th row: Purl.

5th row: Kfb. Knit to end of row.

6th row: Purl.

7th row: Kfb. Knit to last 2 sts. K2tog.

8th row: Purl.

9th row: As 7th row.

10th row: Purl to last 2 sts. Pfb. P1.

11th row: Cast on 8 sts. Knit to last 2 sts. K2tog.

12th row: Purl.

13th row: Knit to last 2 sts. K2tog.

14th row: P2tog. Purl to end of row.

15th row: ssk. Knit to last 2 sts. K2tog.

16th row: Cast off 2 sts. Purl to last 2 sts. P2tog.

17th rows: Cast off 2 sts. Knit to last 2 sts. K2tog.

18th row: Cast off 2 sts. Purl to last 2 sts. P2tog. Cast off.

PILLOW BACK

With MC, cast on 7 sts. Shape bottom of Pillow:

1st row: (WS). Purl.

2nd row: Cast on 2 sts. Knit to last 2 sts. Kfb. K1. 10 sts.

3rd row: Cast on 2 sts. Purl to last 2 sts. Pfb. P1. 13 sts.

4th and 5th rows: As 2nd and 3rd rows. 19 sts.

6th row: As 2nd row. 22 sts.

7th row: Pfb. Purl to last 2 sts. Pfb. P1. 24 sts.

8th row: Kfb. Knit to last 2 sts. Kfb. K1. 26 sts.

9th row: Purl to last 2 sts. Pfb. P1. 27 sts.

10th row: Knit.

11th row: Purl.

12th row: Knit.

13th row: Cast off 4 sts. Purl to last 2 sts. Pfb. P1. 24 sts.

14th row: Knit to last 2 sts. K2tog. 23 sts.

15th row: Cast off 4 sts. Purl to end of row. 19 sts.

16th row: Kfb. knit to last 2 sts. K2tog.

17th row: P2tog. Purl to end of row. 18 sts.

18th row: Knit to last 2 sts. K2tog. 17 sts.

19th row: Purl.

20th row: Knit.

21st row: Purl to last 2 sts. Pfb. P1. 18 sts

22nd row: As 18th row.

Beg on a purl row, work 14 rows stocking st, ending on a knit row.

Shape top of Pillow:

1st row: (WS). Pfb. Purl to end of row.

2nd row: Knit.

3rd row: Purl to last 2 sts. P2tog.

4th row: Knit.

5th row: Pfb. Purl to end of row.

6th row: Knit.

7th row: Pfb. Purl to last 2 sts. P2tog.

8th row: Knit.

9th row: As 7th row.

10th row: Knit to last 2 sts. Kfb. K1.

11th row: Cast on 8 sts. Purl to last 2 sts. P2tog.

12th row: Knit.

13th row: Purl to last 2 sts. P2tog.

14th row: K2tog. Knit to end of row.

15th row: P2tog. Purl to last 2 sts. P2tog.

16th row: Cast off 2 sts. Knit to last 2 sts. K2tog.

17th rows: Cast off 2 sts. Purl to last 2 sts. P2tog.

18th row: Cast off 2 sts. Knit to last 2 sts. K2tog.

Cast off.

Sew Front and Back tog, leaving opening.

Stuff Pillow.

Sew opening closed. Cheek (make 1 for Front only).

With A, cast on 3 sts.

1st row: (WS). (Kfb) twice. K1. 5 sts.

2nd row: Pfb. Purl to last 2 sts. Pfb. P1. 7 sts.

3rd row: Knit. 4th row: As 2nd row. 9 sts.

Beg on a knit row, work 6 rows stocking st.

Next row: (WS). ssk. Knit to last 2 sts. K2tog. 7 sts.

Next row: Purl.

Next row: ssk. Knit to last 2 sts. K2tog. 5 sts.

Next row: P2tog. P1. P2tog.

Cast off.

Sew on Cheek as shown in picture.

With black yarn, embroider eyes as shown in picture.

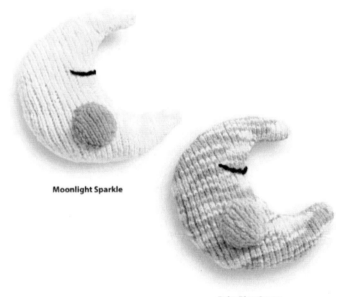

Moonlight Sparkle

Baby Blue Green

IV. Funny Bunny Blanket Hoodie

MATERIALS

Sizes 6/8 10/12 yrs Bernat® Blanket Twist™ (10.5 oz/300 g; 220

yds/201 m)

Main Color (MC) Sea Breeze (57003) 3 balls or 455 yds/414 m 4 balls or 750 yds/683 m

Bernat® Blanket™ (5.3 oz/150 g; 108 yds/98 m) Contrast A

Vintage White (00006) 1 ball or 100 yds/91 m 2 balls or 130 yds/124 m

Size U.S. 11 (8 mm) circular knitting needles 16" [40.5 cm] and 36" [91.5 cm] long or size needed to obtain gauge.

Stitch markers.

Yarn needle.

ABBREVIATIONS

Beg = Begin(ning)

Cont = Continue(ity)

Dec = Decreasing

Inc = Increasing

K = Knit

K2tog = Knit next 2 stitches together

Kfb = Increase 1 stitch by knitting into front and back of next stitch

P = Purl

P2tog = Purl next 2 stitches together

P2togtbl = Purl next 2 stitches together through back of loops

PM = Place marker

Rem = Remain(ing)

Rep = Repeat

RS = Right side

SM = Slip marker

Ssk = Slip next 2 stitches knitwise one at a time. Pass them back onto left-hand needle, then knit through back loops together

St(s) = Stitch(es)

Tog = Together

WS = Wrong side

SIZES

To - t chest measurement

6/8 yrs 25-26½" [63.5-67.5 cm]

10/12 yrs 28-30" [71-76 cm]

Finished chest measurement

6/8 yrs 48" [122 cm]

10/12 yrs 58" [147.5 cm]

GAUGE

8 sts and 13 rows = 4" [10 cm] in stocking st.

INSTRUCTIONS

The instructions are written for smaller size. If changes are necessary for larger size the instruction will be written thus ( ). Numbers for each size are shown in the same color throughout the pattern. When only one number is given in black, it applies to both sizes.

Note: Body of Hoodie is knit in rnds until divide for armholes. Sleeves are picked up from side edge of Body and worked in the rnd towards cu.

BODY

With A and longer circular needle, cast on 90 (110) sts. Join in rnd. PM for beg of rnd.

1st rnd: Purl.

2nd rnd: Knit.

3rd rnd: Purl. Break A.

4th rnd: With MC, [K15 (18). Kfb] 6 times. K0 (2). 96 (116) sts.

Knit in rnds until work from beg measures 17 (20)" [43 (51) cm].

Divide for armholes:

1st row: (RS). K48 (58). Turn. Leave rem sts on a spare needle.

Back:

Beg on a purl row, work in stocking st (Knit on RS rows. Purl on WS

29

rows) on these 48 (58) sts until armhole measures 9 (10)" [23 (25.53) cm], ending on a purl row.

Shape shoulders:

Cast off 8 (10) sts beg next 4 rows. Cast o rem 16 (18) sts.

Front: With RS facing join yarn to rem 48 (58) sts on spare needle and proceed in stocking st until armhole measures 8 rows shorter than Back before beg of shoulder shaping, ending on a purl row.

Shape left neck:

1st row: (RS). K17 (21). K2tog. K1. Turn. Leave rem sts on a spare needle. 19 (23) sts rem.

2nd row: P1. P2tog. Purl to end of row. 18 (22) sts.

3rd row: Knit to last 3 sts. K2tog. K1. 17 (21) sts.

4th row: As 2nd row. 16 (20) sts. Work 4 rows even.

Shape shoulder:

1st row: (RS). Cast o 8 (10) sts. Knit to end of row.

2nd row: Purl. Cast o rem 8 (10) sts.

With MC and RS facing, cast o next 8 (10) sts. Cont on rem 20 (24) sts as follows:

Shape right neck:

1st row: (RS). (You will have 1 st on needle after cast off). ssk. Knit to end of row. 19 (23) sts.

2nd row: Purl to last 3 sts. P2togtbl. P1. 18 (22) sts.

3rd row: K1. ssk. Knit to end of row. 17 (21) sts.

4th rows: As 2nd row. 16 (20) sts. Work 3 rows even.

Shape shoulder:

1st row: (WS). Cast off 8 (10) sts.

Purl to end of row.

2nd row: Knit. Cast o rem 8 (10) sts.

SLEEVES

Sew shoulder seams. With RS facing, MC and shorter circular needle, beg at side between Front and Back, pick up and knit 36 (40) sts evenly around armhole opening.

Join in rnd.

PM for beg of rnd. Knit in rnds until Sleeve measures 10" [25.5 cm]. Break MC. Join A.

Next rnd: With A, *K2tog.

Rep from * around. 18 (20) sts.

Next rnd: Purl.

Next rnd: Knit. Cast o purlwise.

FINISHING

HOOD

With A and longer needle, cast on 45 (49) sts.

Working back and forth in rows across needle, proceed as follows:

Knit 3 rows (garter st), noting 1st row is WS. Break A.

Next row: (RS).

With MC, knit, inc 3 sts evenly across. 48 (52) sts.

Beg on a purl row, proceed in stocking st until work from beg measures 3 (4)" [7.5 (10) cm], ending on a purl row.

Shape neck of Hood:

1st row: (RS). K1. ssk. Knit to last 3 sts. K2tog. K1. 46 (50) sts.

2nd row: P1. P2tog. Purl to last 3 sts. P2togtbl. P1. 44 (48) sts.

3rd and 4th rows: As 1st and 2nd rows. 40 (44) sts.

PM at end of last row.

Beg on a knit row, proceed in stocking st for 10 (12) rows, ending on a purl row.

Shape back of Hood:

1st row: (RS). K18 (20). ssk. PM. K2tog. Knit to end of row. 38 (42) sts.

2nd row: Purl.

3rd row: Knit to 2 sts before marker. ssk. SM. K2tog. Knit to end of row. 36 (40) sts.

4th row: As 2nd row. Rep last 2 rows twice more. 32 (36) sts at end of last row.

Divide sts onto 2 needles.

Graft 2 sets of 16 (18) sts for back seam.

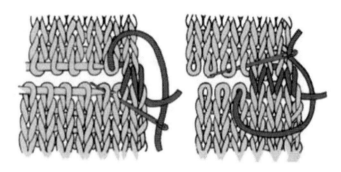

Overlap fronts of Hood at foundation row 1½" [4 cm]. Sew hood around neck opening, matching Hood seam with center back neck edge.

Outer Ears (make 2)

With MC, cast on 8 sts. Work 6 rows stocking st.

Next row: (RS). Kfb. Knit to last 2 sts. Kfb. K1. 10 sts. Work 7 rows stocking st.

Next row: (RS). Kfb. Knit to last 2 sts. Kfb. K1. 12 sts. Cont even until work from beg measures 7 (8)" [18 (20.5) cm], ending on a purl row.

Shape top of Ears:

1st row: (RS). K1. ssk. Knit to last 3 sts. K2tog. K1.

2nd row: Purl.

3rd to 8th rows: As 1st and 2nd rows 3 times more. 4 sts rem.

9th row: (RS). ssk. K2tog.

10th row: P2.

11th row: K2tog. Fasten off.

Inner Ears (make 2)

With A, work as given for Outer Ears.

With WS tog, sew Outer and Inner Ears tog.

Fold foundation row in half.

Sew to Hood as shown in picture.

POCKET

With MC, cast on 28 (32) sts. Proceed in stocking st until work from beg measures 3" [7.5 cm], ending on a purl row.

Shape sides:

1st row: (RS). K3. ssk. Knit to last 5 sts. K2tog. K3.

2nd row: K3. Purl to last 3 sts. K3. Rep last 2 rows 4 (5) times more. 18 (20) sts rem. Cast off.

Try on Hoodie.

Pin Pocket at comfortable height on center front.

Sew Pocket edges in position, leaving shaped sides open.

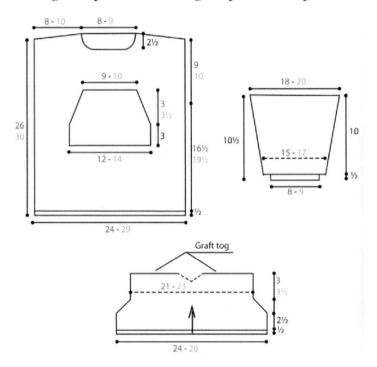

V. Bella & Brian Sloth

MATERIALS

Red Heart® Amigurumi ™ (3.5 oz/100 g; 239 yds/219m) Sloth (9336)

Contrast A Brown

Contrast B Tan

Contrast C Cream

Contrast D Green

1 ball of yarn will make 2 Sloths. 1 ball

Size U.S. 2 (2.75 mm) knitting needles.

Set of 4 size U.S. 2 (2.75 mm) double-pointed needles or size needed to obtain gauge.

Stitch markers.

Four ¼" [6mm] black safety eyes (two per sloth).

Stuffing.

Optional: Four sew-on snap fasteners – size 1 (two per sloth)

ABBREVIATIONS

Approx = Approximately

Beg = Beginning

K = Knit

K2tog = Knit next 2 stitches together

Kfb = Increase 1 stitch by knitting into front and back of next stitch

M1L = Make 1 stitch by picking up horizontal loop from front to back lying before next stitch and knitting into back of loop.

M1R (make 1 right) = Make 1 stitch by picking up horizontal loop from back to front lying before next stitch and knitting into front of loop

PM = Place marker

Rem =Remaining

Rep = Repeat

Rnd(s) = Round(s)

RS = Right side

St(s) = Stitch(es)

Ssk = Slip next 2 stitches knitwise one at a time. Pass them back onto left-hand needle, then knit through back loops together

Tog = Together

WS = Wrong side

W&T = Bring yarn to front of work. Slip next stitch purlwise. Bring yarn to back of work. Slip stitch back onto left-hand needle. Turn. When working the wrapped stitch in next row, pick up the wrap and work it tog with the wrapped stitch.

MEASUREMENT

Approx 6" [15 cm] tall.

GAUGE

25 sts and 32 rows = 4" [10 cm] in stocking st.

INSTRUCTIONS

Note: Before start, separate the different color sections of the yarn as follows:

Push the rings of color out from center.

Find the point where the color changes and cut the yarn.

Rep this process for the rem yarn colors.

Wind each color into a separate ball.

Change to circular knitting needle to accommodate large number of sts when necessary.

BODY/HEAD

Beg at bottom, with A or B and double-pointed needles, cast on 8 sts. Divide onto 3 needles (3, 3, 2).

Join in rnd.

PM for beg of rnd.

1st rnd: (Kfb) 8 times. 16 sts.

2nd rnd: Knit.

3rd rnd: *(K1. M1R) twice. K4. (M1L. K1) twice. Rep from * once more. 24 sts.

4th rnd: Knit.

5th rnd: *(K1. M1R) twice. K8. (M1L. K1) twice. Rep from * once more. 32 sts.

6th rnd: Knit.

7th rnd: *(K1. M1R) twice. K12. (M1L. K1) twice. Rep from * once more. 40 sts.

8th to 13th rnds: Knit. Proceed in rows as follows:

**1st row: (RS). Knit to last 2 sts. W&T.

2nd row: Purl to last 2 sts. W&T.

3rd row: Knit to 1 st before previously wrapped st. W&T.

4th row: Purl to 1 st before previously wrapped st. W&T.

5th and 6th rows: Rep 3rd and 4th rows.

7th row: Knit to end of row, picking up wraps as you go. Do not turn.

8th rnd: Knit around, picking up rem wraps as you go. Do not turn.**

Rep from ** to ** twice more.

Proceed in rnds as follows:

1st to 6th rnds: Knit.

7th rnd: *K1. (ssk) twice. K10. (K2tog) twice. K1. Rep from * once more. 32 sts.

8th to 10th rnds: Knit.

11th rnd: *K1. (ssk) twice. K6. (K2tog) twice. K1. Rep from * once more. 24 sts.

12th to 14th rnds: Knit.

15th rnd: *K1. (ssk) twice. K2. (K2tog) twice. K1. Rep from * once more. 16 sts.

16th to 18th rnds: Knit.

Stuff Body firmly.

19th rnd: *(ssk) twice. (K2tog) twice. Rep from * once more. 8 sts.

Cut yarn, leaving a long end.

Thread end through rem sts. Do not secure the end. You will reopen top of the head to attach the safety eyes when finishing.

LIMBS (make 4)

With A or B, cast on 4 sts. Divide onto 3 needles (1, 1, 2). Join in rnd. PM for beg of rnd.

1st rnd: (Kfb) 4 times. 8 sts.

2nd rnd: Knit.

3rd rnd: *K1. M1R. K2. M1L. K1. Rep from * once more. 12 sts.

4th rnd: Knit.

5th rnd: *K1. M1R. K4. M1L. K1. Rep from * once more. 16 sts.

6th to 13th rnds: Knit.

14th rnd: Ssk. K12. K2tog. 14 sts.

15th to 18th rnds: Knit.

19th rnd: (ssk) twice. K2. M1L. K2. M1R. K2. (K2tog) twice. 12 sts.

20th to 23rd rnds: Knit.

24th rnd: (ssk) twice. K1. M1L. K2. M1R. K1. (K2tog) twice. 10 sts.

25th to 29th rnds: Knit.

Stuff Limb.

30th rnd: Ssk. K6. K2tog. 8 sts.

31st and 32nd rnds: Knit.

33rd rnd: Ssk. K4. K2tog. 6 sts. Break yarn, leaving a long end.

Thread end through rem sts.

Pull tightly.

Fasten securely.

Claws (work 3 claws on each limb)

First claw: With pair of doublepointed needles and C, pick up and knit 2 sts at cast off end of limb, just to the side of center.

Do not turn work. *Slide all sts to opposite end of needle.

Carry yarn tightly across back of work, K2.

Rep from * twice more.

Break yarn, leaving a long end.

Thread end through rem sts.

Pull tightly.

Fasten securely.

Second and third claws: Rep as for First claw, placing Second claw directly over center and Third claw to other side of center.

FACE

With pair of needles and C, cast on 10 sts.

1st row: (WS). Purl.

2nd row: K1. M1R. K8. M1L. K1. 12 sts.

3rd row: Purl.

4th row: K1. M1R. K10. M1L. K1. 14 sts. Beg with a purl row, work 5 rows in stocking st.

Next row: Ssk. Knit to last 2 sts. K2tog. 12 sts.

Next row: Purl. Rep last 2 rows twice more. 8 sts after last row.

Cast off purlwise, leaving a long end for sewing

EYE SPOTS (make 2)

With pair of needles and A, cast on 4 sts. Beg with a purl row, work 3 rows in stocking st.

Next row: (RS). Ssk. K2tog. 2 sts. Break yarn, leaving a long end.

TREE BRANCH (make 1)

With double-pointed needles and D, cast on 8 sts.

Divide onto 3 needles (3, 3, 2) sts.

Join in rnd.

PM for beg of rnd.

Knit in rnds until work from beg measures approx 4" [10 cm].

Break yarn, leaving a long end. Thread end through rem sts.

Pull tightly.

Fasten securely.

TREE LEAF (make as many as desired)

With pair of needles and D, cast on 2 sts.

1st row: (RS). (Kfb) twice. 4 sts.

2nd row: Purl.

3rd row: K1. M1R. K2. M1L. K1. 6 sts.

4th row: Purl. Work 2 rows in stocking st.

Next row: Ssk. K2. K2tog. 4 sts. Beg with a purl row, work 3 rows in stocking st.

Next row: Ssk. K2tog. 2 sts. Break yarn, leaving a long end. Thread end through rem sts. Pull tightly. Fasten securely. Sew leaves to tree branch arranged as desired.

FINISHING

Refer to picture as a guide to placement of face, facial features, and limbs.

Face:

Position face onto body and pin in place. Sew face to body sewing around edges of face and concealing sts as much as possible. Eye Spots:

Position eye spots on face and pin in place. Sew edges of each eye spot onto face.

Nose and Smile:

With A, embroider nose onto face using 3 or 4 straight stitches. Embroider a single straight stitch below nose for smile. Form a bend in smile by sewing a small loop around middle of smile, going out of and back into the same hole.

Eyes: Following manufacturer's instructions, attach safety eyes through each eye spot. Once eyes are secured, thread end through rem sts of head. Pull tightly. Fasten securely.

Limbs:

Note: Sloth's limbs are sewn to body using a loop of yarn pulled tight. This gives the toy a simple joint that allows the limbs to rotate. Position limbs on body and use pins to mark where yarn loop will need to pass through body. Starting with one back leg, sew through inside of leg at widest point. Sew through bottom of body, in one side and out the other, using your pin as a guide. You may need to squeeze body to make this easier. Yarn is now on other side of body. Sew through inside of other leg at widest point. Using pin as a guide, sew back through body. Legs and body are all now connected with one piece of yarn. Twist ends of the yarn together and pull it taut, until legs are pressed firmly to body and body is slightly compressed. Tie a firm square knot.

Pull loose ends of this knot into body. Rep for arms.

Optional: Sew a set of snap fasteners into each pair of paws.

Straight Stitch

VI. Knit Baby Jacket Set

MATERIALS

Bernat® Baby Sport™ (12.3 oz/350 g; 1256 yds/1148 m)

Sizes

Newborn 3 mos 6/12 mos

Baby Grey (21048)

Note: 1 ball makes 3 (2-2) Sets. 1 1 1 ball

Size U.S. 6 (4 mm) circular knitting needle 29" [73.6 cm] long or size needed to obtain gauge.

4 stitch markers.

2 stitch holders.

3 buttons.

ABBREVIATIONS

Alt = Alternate

Approx = Approximate(ly)

Beg = Begin(ning)

K = Knit

K2tog = Knit next 2 stitches together

Kfb = Increase 1 stitch by knitting into front and back loop of next stitch

M1 = Make 1 stitch by picking up loop lying before next stitch and knitting into back of loop

P = Purl

PM = Place marker

Psso = Pass slipped stitch over

Rem = Remaining

Rep = Repeat

RS = Right side

Sl1 = Slip next stitch knitways

SM = Slip marker

Ssk = Slip next 2 stitches knitwise one at a time. Pass them back onto left-hand needle, then knit through back loops together

St(s) = Stitch(es)

WS = Wrong side

SIZES

To fit chest measurement

Newborn 14½" [37 cm]

3 mos 16" [40.5 cm]

6/12 mos 17" [43 cm]

Finished chest

Newborn 17" [44.5 cm]

3 mos 19"[48 cm]

6/12 mos 21" [53.5 cm]

GAUGE

20 sts and 38 rows = 4" [10 cm] in garter st.

INSTRUCTIONS

The instructions are written for smaller size. If changes are necessary for larger size the instructions will be written thus ( ).

Numbers for each size are shown in the same color throughout the pattern.

When only one number is given in black, it applies to both sizes.

Note: Cardigan is worked in one piece from neck edge down. Slip markers as you work.

Beg at neck edge, cast on 52 (56- 60) sts. Do not join.

Working back and forth across needle in rows, proceed as follows:

Neckband: Knit 7 rows (garter st) noting first row is WS.

1st row: (RS). K8 (9-10). M1. PM. K2. PM. M1. K6. M1. PM. K2. PM. M1. K16 (18-20). M1. PM. K2. PM. M1. K6. M1. PM. K2. PM. M1. K8 (9-10). 60 (64-68) sts.

2nd row: (Knit to marker. SM. P2. SM.) 4 times.

Knit to end of row.

3rd row: (Knit to next marker. M1. SM. K2. SM. M1) 4 times.

Knit to end of row. 68 (72-76) sts.

Rep 2nd and 3rd rows 10 (11-11) times more. 148 (160-164) sts.

1st row: (WS). (Knit to next marker. P2) 4 times.

Knit to end of row.

2nd row: (Knit to next marker. K2) 4 times. Knit to end of row.

3rd row:

As 1st row.

4th row: (Knit to next marker. M1. SM. K2. SM. M1) 4 times. Knit to end of row.

Rep last 4 rows 1 (1-2) time(s) more.

164 (176-188) sts.

Next row: (WS). (Knit to next marker. P2) 4 times. Knit to end of row.

Divide Sleeves and Body:

Next row: (RS). K22 (24-26). Slip next 38 (40-42) sts for Sleeve onto st holder. K44 (48-52). Slip next 38 (40-42) sts for Sleeve onto st holder. K22 (24-26). 88 (96-104)sts for Body.

Cont in Garter St until Body from Sleeve divide measures 5 (6-7)" [12.5 (15-18) cm], ending on a RS row.

Cast off knitwise (WS).

Sleeves: With RS facing, rejoin yarn to 38 (40-42) Sleeve sts. Cont in Garter St until work from Body divide measures 4½ (5½-6)" [11.5 (14-15) cm], ending on a RS row.

Cast off knitways (WS).

Sew sleeve seam.

Button Band: Pick up and knit 45 (51-57) sts evenly down left front edge.

Knit 6 rows (garter st).

Cast off knitways (WS).

Place markers on this band for 3 buttons having top button ½" [1 cm] below neck edge, bottom button 4" [10 cm] below top button and rem button centered between.

Buttonhole Band: Pick up and knit 45 (51-57)sts evenly up right front edge. Knit 3 rows (garter st).

Next row: (RS). (Knit to next button marker. K2tog. yo) 3 times. Knit to end of row.

Next 2 rows: Knit. Cast off knitways (WS). Sew on buttons to correspond to buttonholes.

HAT

Cast on 51 (59-69)sts. Do not join.

Working back and forth across needle in rows, proceed as follows:

1st row: (RS). K1. *P1. K1. Rep from * to end of row.

2nd row: *P1. K1. Rep from * to end of row. P1. Rep last 2 rows twice more (6 rows total). Knit in rows (garter st) until work from beg measures 2½ (3-3½)" [6 (7.5-9) cm], ending on a WS row.

Shape top:

1st row: (RS). *K23 (12- 32). K2tog. Rep from * to last 1 (3-1) st(s). K1 (3-1). 49 (55-67) sts.

2nd and alt rows: Knit.

3rd row: K1. *K2tog. K6 (7-9). Rep from * to end of row. 43 (49-61)sts.

5th row: K1. *K2tog. K5 (6-8). Rep from * to end of row. 37 (43-55)sts.

7th row: K1. *K2tog. K4 (5-7). Rep from * to end of row. 31 (37-49)sts.

9th row: K1. *K2tog. K3 (4-6). Rep from * to end of row. 25 (31-43)sts.

11th row: K1. *K2tog. K2 (3-5). Rep from * to end of row. 19 (25-37)sts.

13th row: K1. *K2tog. K1 (2-4). Rep from * to end of row. 13 (19-31)sts.

Sizes 3 mos and 6/12 mos only:

14th row: Knit.

15th row: K1. *K2tog. K (1-3). Rep from * to end of row. (13-25) sts.

Size 6/12 mos only:

16th row: Knit.

17th row: K1. *K2tog. K2. Rep from * to end of row. 19 sts.

All sizes:

Next row: K1. *K2tog. Rep from * to end of row. 7 (7-9)sts.

Break yarn leaving a long end.

Draw end tightly through rem sts.

Sew center back seam.

Ears (make 2)

Cast on 5 sts.

1st row: K5.

2nd row: (Kfb) 4 times. K1. 9 sts. Knit in rows (garter st) until Ear measures 3 (3½-3½)" [7.5 (9-9) cm].

Shape tip:

1st row: K1. K2tog. K3. ssk. K1. 7 sts.

2nd row: Knit.

3rd row: K1. K2tog. K1. ssk. K1. 5 sts.

4th row: Knit.

5th row: K1. Sl1. K2tog. psso. K1. 3 sts.

6th row: Knit.

7th row: Sl1. K2tog. psso.

Fasten off.

Fold cast on edge in half and sew Ears in position to Hat as shown in photo.

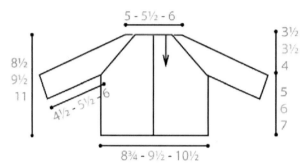

VII. Cutie Booties And Cap To Knit

MATERIALS

Bernat® Baby Sport™ (12.3 oz/350 g; 1256 yds/1148 m)

Baby Gray (21048) or Baby Pink (21420) 1 ball

Note: 1 ball makes 9 Sets of Bootees and Cap.

Set of 5 size U.S. 5 (3.75 mm) double-pointed knitting needle or size needed to obtain gauge.

Stitch markers.

ABBREVIATIONS

Alt = Alternate

Approx = Approximate(ly)

Beg = Begin(ning)

Cont = Continue(ity)

Dec = Decrease(ing)

Inc = Increase(ing)

K = Knit

Kfb = Increase 1 stitch by knitting into front and back of next stitch

K2(3)tog = Knit next 2(3) stitches together

P = Purl

Pat = Pattern

PM = Place marker

Psso = Pass slipped stitch over

Rem = Remain(ing)

Rep = Repeat

Rnd(s) = Round(s)

RS = Right side

Sl1 = Slip next stitch knitwise

SM = Slip marker

Ssk = Slip next 2 stitches knitwise one at a time. Pass them back onto left-hand needle, then knit through back loops together.

St(s) = Stitch(es)

WS = Wrong side

Yo = Yarn over

SIZE

One size to fit baby 6-12 months

GAUGE

23 sts and 32 rows = 4" [10 cm] in stocking st.

INSTRUCTIONS

BOOTIES

Note: Sole is worked in rows using 2 needles.

Rem of Bootee is worked in the rnd using set of 5 needles.

Sole: With pair of needles, cast on 6 sts.

1st row: (WS). Knit.

2nd row: Kfb. Knit to last 2 sts. Kfb. K1. 8 sts.

3rd to 6th rows: Rep last 2 rows twice more. 12 sts.

7th to 33rd rows: Knit.

34th row: K1. K2tog. Knit to last 3 sts. K2tog. K1. 10 sts.

35th row: Knit.

36th to 39th rows: Rep last 2 rows twice more. 6 sts.

Proceed as follows:

Instep: With RS facing and using rem needles, pick up and knit 18 sts down side of Sole, 4 sts across cast on edge of Sole and 18 sts up other side of Sole.

Join in rnd.

Sts are divided as: 6 sts on first needle, 18 sts on 2nd needle, 4 sts on 3rd needle, 18 sts on 4th needle.

PM on first st. 46 sts.

1st rnd: Purl.

2nd to 7th rnds: Knit. Place marker on needle between 26th and 27th sts (center of toe).

8th rnd: Knit to 6 sts before marker. (K2tog) 3 times. SM. (K2tog) 3 times.

Knit to end of rnd. 40 sts.

9th rnd: Knit.

10th to 13th rnds: Rep 8th and 9th rnds twice more. 28 sts.

Cuff:

Next rnd: *K1. P1. Rep from * around.

Rep last rnd until cuff measures 3" [7.5 cm].

Cast off in ribbing.

CAP

Cast on 82 sts.

Divide sts on 4 needles (20, 20, 20, 22).

Join in rnd.

PM on first st.

1st rnd: *K1. P1. Rep from * around. Rep last rnd 7 times more (8 rnds total), inc 1 st in center of last rnd. 83 sts. Knit 2 rnds.

Place Lace Heart Chart:

Next rnd: K35. Work 1st row of Lace Heart chart across next 13 sts. K35. Lace Heart chart is now in position. Cont working Lace Heart chart until 15 rows of chart are complete. Knit in rnds until work from beg measures 4½" [11.5 cm], dec 3 sts evenly across last rnd. 80 sts.

Shape top:

1st rnd: *K6. K2tog. ssk. K6. Rep from * 4 times more. 70 sts.

2nd and alt rnds: Knit.

3rd rnd: *K5. K2tog. ssk. K5. Rep from * 4 times more. 60 sts.

5th rnd: *K4. K2tog. ssk. K4. Rep from * 4 times more. 50 sts.

7th rnd: *K3. K2tog. ssk. K3. Rep from * 4 times more. 40 sts.

9th rnd: *K2. K2tog. ssk. K2. Rep from * 4 times more. 30 sts.

11th rnd: *K1. K2tog. ssk. K1. Rep from * 4 times more. 20 sts.

13th rnd: *K2tog. ssk. Rep from * 4 times more. 10 sts.

Break yarn leaving a long end.

Draw end tightly through rem sts.

Lace Heart Chart

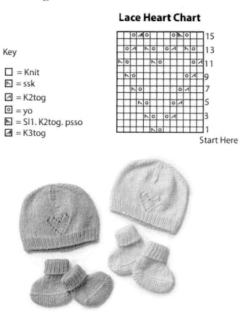

Key

☐ = Knit
ℕ = ssk
◪ = K2tog
☉ = yo
ℕ = Sl1. K2tog. psso
◪ = K3tog

Start Here

VII. Strawberry Set

SIZE: 6 mos, 12 mos, 18 mos, 24 months (2 yrs), Child 3

CARDIGAN

Finished Chest 20 (21, 23, 24, 26) in. (51 (53.5, 58.5, 61, 66) cm)

Finished Length 9 1/2 (11, 12, 13, 14) in. (24 (28, 30.5, 33, 35.5) cm)

HAT S (M, L)

Finished Circumference 13 (15, 17) in. (33 (38, 43) cm)

Note: Pattern is written for smallest size with changes for larger sizes in parentheses. When only one number is given, it applies to all sizes. To follow pattern more easily, circle all numbers pertaining to your size before beginning.

MATERIALS

821-101 Lion Brand Superwash Merino Cashmere

Yarn: Blossom 5 6, 7, 8, 9 Balls

Lion Brand Knitting Needles- Size 8 [5 mm]

Lion Brand Split Ring Stitch Markers

Lion Brand Stitch Holders

Large-Eye Blunt Needles (Set of 6)

Additional Materials 3 buttons, 5/8 in. (16 mm) diameter

NOTE To make Hat only, you will need 1 (1, 2) balls of yarn.

GAUGE

17 sts + 34 rows = 4 in. (10 cm) in Garter st (k every row). BE SURE TO CHECK YOUR GAUGE. When you match the gauge in a

pattern, your project will be the size specified in the pattern and the materials specified in the pattern will be sufficient.

If it takes you less stitches and rows to make a 4 in. [10 cm] square, try using a smaller size hook or needles; if more stitches and rows, try a larger size hook or needles.

ABBREVIATIONS

beg = begin(s)(ning)

k = knit

k2tog = knit 2 together

rep = repeat(s)(ing)

RS = right side st(s) = stitch(es)

WS = wrong side

yo = yarn over

NOTES: Yoke and sleeves are knit in one piece, from sleeve cuff to sleeve cuff. Stitches are then picked up along lower edges of yoke for back and fronts.

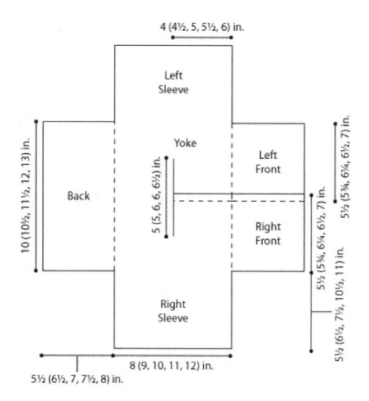

INSTRUCTIONS

CARDIGAN

Yoke and Sleeves Beg at right sleeve cuff, cast on 34 (40, 44, 48, 52)
sts.

Work in Garter st (k every row) until piece measures 5 1/2 (6 1/2, 7
1/2, 10 1/2, 11) in. (14 (16.5, 19, 26.5, 28) cm) from beg. Place markers
at beg and end of last row for placement of back and fronts.

Continue in Garter st until piece measures 2 1/2 (2 3/4, 2 3/4, 3, 3 1/4) in. (6.5 (7, 7, 7.5, 8.5) cm) from markers. Divide for Neck

Next Row (RS): K17 (20, 22, 24, 26) sts for right front yoke and place these sts on a holder, k across remaining 17 (20, 22, 24, 26) sts for back yoke.

Back Yoke

Working over back yoke sts only, continue in Garter st until piece measures 5 (5, 6, 6, 6 1/2) in. (12.5 (12.5, 15, 15, 16.5) cm) from beg of neck divide, end with a WS row. Place back yoke sts on holder.

Right Front Yoke

From WS, place right front yoke sts back onto needle, join yarn and continue in Garter st until piece measures 2 1/2 (2 1/2, 3, 3, 3 1/4) in. (6.5 (6.5, 7.5, 7.5, 8.5) cm) from beg of neck divide, end with a WS row. Next Row (buttonholes - RS): *K3 (4, 4, 5, 5), yo, k2tog (for buttonhole); rep from * 2 more times, k to end. Knit 3 rows.

Bind off.

Left Front Yoke

Cast on 17 (20, 22, 24, 26) sts. Work in Garter st until piece measures 3 (3, 3 1/2, 3 1/2, 3 3/4) in. (7.5 (7.5, 9, 9, 9.5) cm) from beg, end with a WS row.

Join Left Front and Back Yokes

Joining Row (RS): Knit across left front yoke sts, knit across back yoke sts on holder - 34 (40, 44, 48, 52) sts at the end of this row. Work even in Garter st until piece measures 2 1/2 (2 3/4, 2 3/4, 3, 3 1/4) in. (6.5 (7, 7, 7.5, 8.5) cm) from joining row. Place markers at beg and end of last row for placement of back and fronts.

Work even in Garter st until piece measures 5 1/2 (6 1/2, 7 1/2, 10 1/2, 11) in. (14 (16.5, 19, 26.5, 28) cm) from markers.

Bind off.

Back

With RS facing, pick up and k42 (44, 48, 52, 56) sts evenly spaced between markers along lower edge of back yoke.

Work even in Garter st for 5 1/2 (6 1/2, 7, 7 1/2, 8) in. (14 (16.5, 18, 19, 20.5) cm).

Bind off.

Fronts

With RS facing, pick up and k24 (25, 27, 29, 31) sts evenly spaced along lower edge of one front yoke edge between marker and front edge.

Work even in Garter st until same length as back.

Bind off.

Repeat along other front yoke edge.

FINISHING

Fold piece in half along shoulders. Sew side and sleeve seams.

Sew buttons to left front opposite buttonholes.

Weave in ends.

Hat

Cast on 56 (64, 72) sts.

Work even in Garter st (k every row) until piece measures 4 (4 1/2, 5) in. (10 (11.5, 12.5) cm) from beg.

Shape Top of Hat

Row 1: *K2tog; rep from * to end of row - 28 (32, 36) sts at the end of this row.

Row 2: Knit. Rep last 2 rows 2 more times - 7 (8, 9) sts remain. Cut yarn, leaving a 16 in. (40.5 cm) tail.

Thread tail through remaining sts and pull to gather.

Use remaining tail to sew back seam.

Made in United States
North Haven, CT
10 December 2023

45499823R10039